At Large

Graeme Hetherington

At Large

Acknowledgement is due to the following publications
in which these poems first appeared:
The Age, *Antipodes*, *Blue Dog*, *The Canberra Times*, *Five Bells*,
The Mozzie, *Poetry For Public Transport*, *Poetry Matters*,
Quadrant, *Southerly*, *Studio*, *The Sydney Morning Herald*,
The Tasmanian Review, *Valley Micropress* (NZ),
The Weekend Australian, *Westerly*.

At Large
ISBN 978 1 76041 422 1
Copyright © text Graeme Hetherington 2017
Cover image: *At Large*, painting by Terry O'Malley

First published 2017 by
GINNINDERRA PRESS
PO Box 3461 Port Adelaide 5015 Australia
www.ginninderrapress.com.au

Contents

One	7
Voyage	9
Two	11
London	13
After Francis Bacon's *Triptych 1970*	17
Palmesel	18
Three	19
Athens	21
Parthenon	28
Music to my Ears	31
In the Image of Gods	32
Four	33
Crete	35
On the Waterfront, Hania, Crete	39
For Michael Winters	42
Five	43
Arrivals and Departures in Italy	45
Florence	47
The Ghost of Dante, Ravenna	51
Death in Venice	52
Six	57
Retiro Park, Madrid	59
The Escorial	63
Toledo	64
Avila	69
For St John of the Cross, Segovia	71

Seven	**73**
Istanbul	75
Through the Eyes of Gallipoli	78
Three Hittite Kings	82
Eight	**85**
With James McAuley and Georg Trakl in Vienna	87
Hotel Terminus, Vienna	90
Vienna	91
Rembrandt's Self-portraits in Vienna	93
After a Painting by Matisse	94
Mediaeval German Christs	95
Nine	**97**
Former Czech Communist Boss	99
Czech Republic	100
Czech Concert	101
Jack the Ripper in Prague	102
Winter Walk, Hradec Králové	103
Ten	**105**
Constitutional	107
Dance of Death: Binalong Bay	108
Memento Mori at Seventy-eight	110
East Coast, Tasmania (2)	111

One

Voyage

(After Cavafy)

The ticket's condition is clear:
No turning back on the voyage
You didn't even choose to take,
And which, though short, is longest, since

It shadows and incorporates
All. Fearful, you can change wives, work,
Your house, country, real ships, and go
Anywhere whenever you like,

In actuality or dream,
Believe you are dodging your fate,
And still you're chained to time that needs
No relieving shift at the helm,

So constantly intent is it
On getting you there as programmed.
You can have one of heart – a change,
That is – becoming Death's best friend

By loving black in every form,
Hoping to be spared when at last
You sail into port, options gone,
As trapped as you were at the first.

Two

London

1

Who are we that we shorten day
And arrogantly gain ten hours
As ever-youthfully we speed?
The plastic tickets with our names

Engraved in thick black bubble-print
The ultimate in credit cards
Computerised to see us through
The never-ending empty night.

2

The carpenters came unannounced,
Removed a door and left a hole
To guard us from the outside world.
We slept in perfect peace that night,

For who could cross a pit so wide,
Climb back from anywhere so deep,
Or penetrate a wall as thick
As darkness in a hotel hall?

3

We walk this city and its parks,
Its stone-hard monumental streets
That thrust like lovers to their goal
Beyond the pitch-black iron gates,

Disperse as gentle garden paths
Among the grass-soft beds of bulbs,
Or arch as anxious question marks
Across the weed-dark lily ponds.

4

She knows my visiting won't last
And asks why I can't live with them.
The TV holds her more than my

Evasive, vague reply, until
I think we'll easily say goodbye.
But as I fasten up my stiff

Coat buttons, agitated six
Year old fingers insist I'm wrong
And tug them violently undone.

5

(for Edward VIII)

It is my task as friend to say
'Stay true to her and abdicate,
Don't be the traitor-king they want!

My need to look up to a god-
Like human on this earth is strong,
My expectations high and not

To be denied.' And when he chose
For love I cheered and loudly cried
'The worst is dead long live the best!'

6

The flame-haired fallen angels live
As punk kids in the Underground,
As pathless comets through the night
In jet-black silver-studded clothes,

While Lucifer with dead-white face
And scarlet plume's a bloodshot moon,
A scythe to cut a way through crowds
And lead them moth-like up the stairs.

7

From our inner-city refuge,
For two weeks, the light, like our towels
And bed linen, has been unchanged.
At any time it could be dawn
About to break or dusk that falls,

The silence grown as final as
A death. You have to go outside
To learn of steady rain, to crave
For all the seasons to occur
As in one mad Tasmanian day.

After Francis Bacon's *Triptych 1970*

He has shown, perhaps with a damp,
Booze-steadied hand, two men as they
Confront each other from the wings.

Sophisticated Londoners,
Their cultivated elegance
And casualness of pose belie

The fear of having gone too far
In searching out the prospects for
Illicit sex. Sly knowing grins

Suddenly checked and frozen in
A rictus like silk curtains rucked
Halfway across, it is the lull

Before the storm, soul sickening for
The flesh, the beast about to pounce.
And the release is a collapse

Into the centre, where limbs twined,
Voraciously enmeshed suggest,
Not love, but murder being done.

Palmesel

(Queen Victoria and Albert Museum)

1

Gentle donkey, gentle man
Welcomed by enormous crowds
Eager to be cured with hope,

They will later turn and show
Love's not easy to sustain,
That the donkey was His friend.

2

From the dreadful hurt of life,
From the frightful outrage done
Comes a sense of horror at

Existence in its human form,
Comes the need to hope and pray
God at least might understand.

Three

Athens

1

From puritan Paul's Corinth, where
He'd passionately hammered home
His 'truth' that only abstinence
From sex gave purity and hope
Of immortality, I came

One hot day to Athens, a death-
Fouled city from pollution of
Another kind, since car fumes, not
Their seats convertible to beds,
Now guaranteed a dirty end.

2

Beneath a neon-lit beer glass,
Alternately replenished, drained,
Repeatedly without a pause,
Men shouting about politics
Froth at the mouth and jump around,

Torn as they are between the need
To get a word in edgeways, or
To take a pee, while in doorways
Drunkards awakening see the sign
And topped up pass out blind again.

3

Since Paris taught Greeks not to trust
Foreign guests, respect for the law
Of hospitality ordained
By Zeus has fallen off. Now mass

Tourism deals the *coup de grâce*
As hosts seize every chance to cheat,
As though it were the last they had
To even up the score before

Capricious history strikes again,
Perhaps this time with loss worse than
Of peerless Helen, or of life
The ten-year war for her brought on.

4

Old tourists live mostly indoors,
Swivelling stands with postcards to view
Their new world. They drink in air-cooled,
Golden-lit bars, or round a pool

They seldom use, though it's enclosed
By perspex walls temptingly blue
As untroubled sky and calm sea.
Crinkled in parts with yellow lines

To show sun and beaches, they're like
Four huge packages gift-wrapped in
Cellophane that's both baby-smooth
And wrinkled as skin that has aged.

5

The puce-gloved, dancing-master styled,
Near-Chaplinesque, hereditary
Greek dermatologist waltzed in,
Peeled off the kid that he might choose

From three holes in my nose the one
In need of lasering. That done,
He tripped the light fantastic, as,
Calling on Zeus, he hurled a bolt,

Which came less from that simple god
With fixed target in mind, than from
The much more complicated cult
Of Lachrymose Christi, since though

The treatment healed, it also caused
Both eyes to weep and thus replaced
The open wound with two that look
Like oysters I find hard to shut.

6

Discharged, alone and broke, I was,
With clumsily dressed nose, reduced
In streets named for Euripides,
Aristophanes, Aeschylus

And Sophocles, to sniffing round
As tragicomic clown among
The poorer sorts of prostitutes
Soliciting that winter night

In pants and bra, to hoping that
One might fall, like me, victim to
The simple need for human warmth,
So strong that money didn't count.

7

My world today a park's iron bench
Of strips wrought into circles with
Wide gaps between, the pine grown through,
Its limbs well-trimmed, is like a top's

Extended handle Zeus pumps with,
Invisibly, spinning the whole
As fast as earth to keep me safe.
But housed next door in ruins, his

Once monumental temple built
By Hadrian, he might decide,
Piqued by our long neglect, to rest
His hand and fling me to the wolves.

8

Far from retreating because of
The total loss of flakes at first,
The snow persisted till it firmed

And Athens had gone under, save
Of course for olive trees, still seen
As sacrosanct and left to breathe,

And this though they had failed to bring
About even the shortest of
Cease-fires. Instead leaves lost their shine

And turned as sallow as the Greeks,
Blood drained by what was usually not
Thought worth the bother to fight off,

To find and wear rotten-from-no-
Use gumboots and man broken old
Garden shovels on account of,

But which, nevertheless, once in
A blue moon, insistently storms,
Invades in depth and purifies.

Parthenon

1

The Parthenon breaks up and lies
Condemned to death beneath a sky
That's not been blue for sixty years,
But like the ceiling of a house

That's warped and buckled by the smoke
Might fall and bury lesser rooms
Like temples on the tops of hills,
Or so invade and crush the minds

Of those Athena should protect
The goddess will be driven out,
Denied the only shrine that counts
And made to breathe the city air.

2

Armed guards patrol the entrances
And scaffolding retains the walls,
The fractured underlying rock
That once reared like a beast they tamed

In honour of a virgin's shrine.
Now straying, rampant billy goats
That mock with wicked, yellow eyes
Defoliate the olive trees,

3

Like bits of skeleton exposed,
The hilltop shrine means nothing more
Than money to the modern Greeks
Whose ancient namesakes worshipped there.

Disoriented sons of Turks,
They sleep on moonlit, windy nights
While ghosts of disinterred remains
Beg mournfully for deeper graves.

4

Because her home has been deflowered
The virgin-goddess has withdrawn
Her favour from the people's lives.
Pollution will destroy their health,

Hard-core pornography their souls
Until her purity's restored,
Her stone-white images allowed
To flower once more before their eyes.

5

The columns open to the light,
The Parthenon's a honeycomb
Where swarms of students come to store
The golden homage of their souls,

Its fractured stones a music score
Too new and difficult for Zeus,
But joyfully the younger gods
Are listening to the modern song.

Music to my Ears

'Petros Petridis, Symphony',
Whose number and defining key
I now forget, but there it was
In black and white on posters stuck
On Athen's downtown concert hall,

An old friend famous for the work
He'd dedicated himself to.
Back in the nineteen-sixties, for
The time it took to have a snack
In Kolonaki restaurants,

He'd join his loneliness to mine.
'I've proved you can get music from
A stone', he joked in reference to
His name. *Notes From The Underworld*
Obtruding from coat pocket gave

His bona fides, black beret
And bow tie his Parisian
Credentials. 'Ugly as a toad,'
He said into a mirror once,
'Small wonder I love Socrates!'

I bought a single ticket, heard,
Prepared by having known him, clear,
Distinctly separated notes
Establishing the true pure hell
Of life as always being lone.

In the Image of Gods

Achilles said he hated like Hell's Gates
His god-sanctioned lord who said one thing
And hid another in his heart.

He is the first idealist of the kind
Who wanted honesty as stark as his own heart,
Who would have slain Agamemnon

But for the gods who wisely ruled
In favour of the outward show
And blessed him with a touch of hell.

Four

Crete

1

I can't abide Dalmatian hounds,
The way they're spotted black and white,
Or even mottled mountainsides
As sunlight melts the winter snow,

But if the rent is really low,
The town upon the coast of Crete,
I tolerate terrazzo floors
That sniff around my ankle bones.

2

The sun-forged, sea-cooled stone of myth
Now gives off dust instead of mist
As concrete workers patch and seal,
Bulldoze the labyrinths and caves
For lesser gods who buy their fame

With villas in the worn-out hills
Where out-of-date old Daedalus
In eyeshade bent across his board
Still roughs out wings for Icarus
And houses Zeus among the clouds.

3

To mend a house they improvise
With anything that comes to hand,
Leftovers from the time before:
A piece of rotten string or wire

To keep a sheet of tin in place,
A chip of wood to plug a hole
That widens as it's being fixed,
Or splintered stick to prop a wall

Since nothing is too old to save
And only money can't be found.
The concrete mixer is their god
And comes at the eleventh hour.

4

I asked when they'd clean up the town,
The garbage that carpets the streets,
The fallen down homes and old bones
Of dogs starved to death on the chain,
The half-witted government clerks

With one little fingernail long
To prove they don't do any work.
The General gained victory with words:
'We'll wait to be cleaned up again
By Germans, Italians or Turks.'

5

The winter mountains clad like gods
In snow that only fell last night
Stand suddenly much closer to
A town still occupied with war,

Besieging with a stronger light
And fresher air the ruined streets
And fortress walls, as though they want
Before the thaw and their retreat

Into the plains, to liberate
From memories the TPIs
And widows always dressed in black
Who barely offer them a glance.

6

The farmyard's à la modern Crete
With fowls that roost in olive trees,
Lay eggs in any soft warm place
Like children who aren't toilet trained.
The half-a-dozen sheep and goats

With nothing left to nibble at
Move clumsily among the stones.
A chained-up pig melts in the sun
While rabbits copulate and lose
All sense of classical restraint.

7

Desiring only peace, I sit,
A monster of sloth in the cool
Subaqueous shade of the park,
A latter-day Tiamat in

Her role of the annual spring flood
In Mesopotamia, or,
More correctly, its aftermath,
Stagnating with hate as I watch

My foe, the world's creator, god-
King Marduk as head gardener rush
Around, utilising me on
Loathed civilisation's behalf

And soaking summer-withered lawns.
But when, wanting something to do,
With violent assertion and noise,
He next becomes, provoked by my

Extreme passivity, a boy
With water pistol squirting till
My eyes are running like the twin
Rivers, Tigris and Euphrates,

I, stirred to the depths, overcome
Inertia and can't wait to rise,
To inundate again, and this
Time wipe life from the face of earth.

On the Waterfront, Hania, Crete

1

A lone old man, I watch as waves
Curl lips, and, salivating, spill,
Near youths disporting on baked rocks

Until they dive off for relief.
Emerging sleekly, glistening like
Porpoises bobbing through the sea's

Tight velvet sheen, they wear it torn
And slipping off as they climb back,
As soothed as a burnt finger sucked

And dragged along the inside of
A cheek and then popped slowly out,
Spit stretched so thin in strands it snaps

And fails to even faintly film.
At lunch – as fresh as fruit just picked,
That yearns, for all we know, for mouths

Before it's overripe – they ache
In bodies longing for release,
Kiss-eat, caress each other, sigh,

Preparing for siesta, when,
Limbs sweetly racked to breaking point,
They'll die the little death at last.

2

A pitch-black Emil Nolde sea
With intermittent flash of white
As summer fades and night brings in
The cold for those like me who've seen

The tourists out to walk alone
And wonder why this scene should now
Evoke his work, when at about
This time for weeks I've passed it by

Without even a thought: the hordes
My company then that took the chill
Off loneliness, I needed in
My loss to find another friend.

3

Moonlight laddering a harbour swell
Too deeply to see where, or if
It ended, I wanted to save
The wavering scene from flickering out.

And as I gazed, thinking the last,
The lowest rung must be the first,
The earliest sent down, I found
Myself in childhood's mirror of

Unfathomable, black despair,
Eyes needing to shut tight and rest
Giving but a faint afterglow
Of steps to climb before I drowned.

For Michael Winters

Your drawings catch the cutting light,
Reveal the Cretans as relaxed,
Reclining carelessly in streets
As full of twists and broken lines

As their long history's fractured with
Duplicity, mistrust and war,
Or leaning in stone doorways wrenched
And bent by time into all shapes,

Against warped windows crucified
As though it were their natural right,
Your lone Australian soldier raw,
New-looking in his uniform

As tripping on the cobblestones
He sheepishly gawks round, exposed
As out of place beneath the slouch
Set stiffly on his youthful head.

Five

Arrivals and Departures in Italy

1

(Aeneas laments the drowning of his helmsman)

'The fickle gods in sparing us from Troy
And Dido's rage disguised the snares of hope.
The quieter seas spoke softly on and on:'
'Time now to trust and heed the god of sleep,

To seek release and free homecoming minds
From waking dreams of murder, rape and worse.'
'O Palinurus, well-read in heaven's signs,
You watched until the sea beguiled your wits.'

2

The sun a raw wound over Greece
Predicting yet another coup,
Reflected in the waterways
Of Yugoslavia it looked
Like organised collection points

For recent spillages of blood.
But, golden above Italy,
And haloing, as we arrived,
The fields of cut-back, cross-shaped vines,
It was more abstract and refined.

3

The sadness of Italy is in its trains,
The railway stations with high ceilings, dark
And with an overhanging chill.
There seem fewer welcomings than goodbyes.

At Florence, an old man sat down with his thoughts,
His face a script where all of history might be read.
A woman greeted him and he smiled like the sun.
The happiness of Italy is in its trains.

4

Reception's coldly fleeting smile
Is welcome and goodbye in one
For folk booked in for just the night.
The foyer Christmas tree agrees,

Encouraging the stop-go rate
To escalate with red and green
Lights flashing on and off without
An orange glow between to give

At least a pause for thought about
A change of mind and staying on,
As though Death can be dodged, such is
The mania to quickly move.

Florence

1

Bare terracotta walls, except
For light and shadow playing there,
The silence of clay water-jug,

Bowls, platters, welcoming fruit, tense
With longing for the ancient gods
To find them worthy of their use,

Morandi could have painted this
Still life that hushes us, afraid
To enter and enjoy our room.

2

In Santa Croce square a crowd
Drugged dreamy-eyed and sweat-filmed shouts
For peace on earth to be restored.
Inside the church damp flaking bits
Of fresco claimed to be 'Christ's Life'

By Giotto shrivel up and wince,
As though ashamed to hear again,
Still unrequited, the demand,
And faintly echoing the cry
Lend their support until the end.

3

(Bargello Museum)

A rearing dragon sharpens claws on stone,
Its jaw dropped down for tongues of fire to pour
On ravening lions and soaring birds of prey,

Ghibellines and Guelphs feuding to this day.
The steady sun, the sky's great coat of arms
Cracks stone and smooths the savagery of men.

4

(Pope Boniface VIII: after Arnolfo di Cambio)

He kicked a kneeling envoy in the face.
The wiser thought him better locked away
And then to save his image if they could.
Perhaps they thought the sculptor served them well:

Straight-backed in stone, he could be taken as divine.
Tapering upwards, surely he aspires,
Yet tightly drawn in he's rigid with control,
The left boot jutting from the base.

5

The people move haphazardly around,
Compete with cars on crossings and in alley-ways.
The young ones train their motor bikes to rear,
But churches here serve sanity like parks

And the cathedral's mercifully at hand.
Castagno's rider struggling with his mount,
I'm thankful for the peace Uccello gives,
His horse and soldier completely in accord.

6

The Arno, thick and still from silt
Seems just as much a bridge as those
With fluent stone grain crossing it
Are rivers rippling, eddying,
Both swift and slow, according to

The tempo of the traffic's one-
Way flow, while arches roared through by
It are like waves about to break,
And would, save for the perching birds
Strained heavenwards before they fly.

7

From tottering cardinals in their brilliant dress
To half-wits clearing tourists from a church,
Here everything is openly on view:

Red white and green torn bits of paper caught
On trees above the waterline,
The river hangs its washing out.

The Ghost of Dante, Ravenna

'An aged sacristan, who used to sleep in that part of the building, was accustomed to tell of seeing in dreams a figure clad in red, who issued from the wall and passed through the chapel…' – Dorothy L. Sayers

Tonight I didn't rise in rage-
Red, soaking-wet doctoral robes,
Perversely pretending it was
To vary the sacristan's dreams

And startle the wits out of monks
Asleep at their pre-dawn prayers,
When Jacopo, my poet-son,
But second-rate, had caused the sweat

To break out in my soul enraged
At his attempts to recompose
My 'lost' thirteen cantos. Instead,
I passed as dry as a bone, clean

As a whistle through the tomb's lid,
My agony resolved at last.
And now, wrung out to truth, sun up,
I'm fit to give the blessing of

Good news, show where I hid them for
The boy to have a chance to share
In my posterity if he
Were equal to enhancing it.

Death in Venice

1

San Marco's gold has lost its gleam,
And miserable in mist the doge
Foscari kneels in stone before
Two badly weathered dripping lions,
While workmen laying planks above

Tide's record-breaking reach point at
Reflections of old palaces
That sag and waver even more
Upon the water's face, shake heads
That seem to say 'next time for sure'.

2

Grey feathery drenched cathedral domes
Look like emus sheltering beneath
Wings otherwise without a use,
A heaviness echoed throughout

The spreading press of stone. Inside
Barbaric gold and rubies light
A man-sized Father, Son and Ghost
Once ruled by doges living near:

Too close for comfort for souls less
Materialistic, though bells,
As now, would have rung out their flocks
Of silvery notes that fly beyond.

3

(Doge's Palace)

Late evening light discolours with
The truth, revealing gilded wings
Of lions and angels peeling back
To sickening seaweed-green against
The sinisterly cobweb-grey

And purple-as-a-bruise facade
Whose pitted texture slimes the mix,
The cruelty and intrigue beneath
The smear of piety breaking out
Like a disease upon the skin.

4

The rising Grand Canal drowned streets,
Confining us indoors to dredge
From memory and transmute our finds
To images in sketches, words,

Wondering all the time about
The angel in the square below
Our window we by leaning out
Could touch as she turned on her tower.

Like us she seemed glad to be high
And dry, surveying to recall
Without having to risk her wings,
Outspread in gold to equate with

Our flights of imagination.
Or had she just flown in to view
From the best vantage point her work
Of widening catastrophe,

Leaving her pinions at full span
That she might crow and glory as
Triumphal Messenger of Death
And Mistress of the watery grave?

5

A plaque set high up on a wall reminds
That two hundred Jews of six million killed
Came from here. Near the abattoirs we see

A huge Alsatian with his muzzle off.
I feel ashamed with blue eyes and grey hair,
Walking here in sunlight cold beyond belief.

6

The dust has won out in these rooms
Where crumbling tapestries and spine-broken books
Are holy relics proudly kept

By the curator, an asthmatic, shuffling Jew,
Who has his desert, if not his Promised Land,
The window dirty, leaves clinging to a tree.

Six

Retiro Park, Madrid

1

The sandy avenues are named
Argentina, Paraguay, Peru,
Their full-grown flanking pines and planes

Cut savagely to cactus shapes,
The gardeners straightening from their work
To five foot miracles of growth.

2

Triangles, circles, rhomboids, squares,
The garden's formal and precise,
Coldly abstract and severe,

A place to burn men at the stake,
The wrought-iron polished rubbish bins
Unrelentingly ideal.

3

Here nature has been brought to heel
With trees and hedges clipped to shapes
The soldier-kings on pedestals approve,
The sky a pearl-grey lacquered dome,

Its borders painted pink and gold
To make the world a drawing room
For fey Alonso to take snuff
Or sniff the air for something wrong.

4

An old man searches rubbish bins
And red and silver coke cans gleam
In black mud tracked across the grass.
The trees are threadbare with last leaves,

Moth-eaten looking in their spread,
Egg-yellow staining dull grey bark,
While mist around the sculptures re-
Creates the Royals in beggars' clothes.

5

The knock-kneed kings in flaky stone
Have slender hands on drooping wrists,
Raise eyebrows, pirouette and sigh

In melodramas of defeat.
A nearby gutted tree trunk sways,
Discards the last of seven veils.

6

Men died here, fighting from behind
Thick oaks, whose wet leaves working in
To mounds of earth suggest shared graves,
If little else, to judge from tight-
Lipped veterans marching back and forth

In their bemedalled best. Heads bowed
In thought, they seem unable to
Shrug off, inter survivors' guilt,
The past that clings and rots, while trees
In weeping shed and bury theirs.

7

The legacies of poverty and war,
The Goya-face and crippled limb,
Velazquez's idiot and drunk
Move past the statues of the kings

And seem like members of a court
Ruled by an inbred lantern jaw,
Poor silly Charles with heavy arse
An ostrich backing through a door.

8

A face as slippery, fat and bland
As oysters soaked in oil spits up
A gob of phlegm onto the path,
The huge havana flicked and sniffed,

Jammed like a turd into his mouth,
While Charles the second limply stands,
Fly buttons bulging in soft stone,
Near still pond water glazed with scum.

9

The city's thrusting, vigorous and new,
With steel and plastic flowers instead
Of wrought iron balcony and rose,

The fine-boned members of the past
Consigned with lilac-coloured lamps
To keep Charles company in the park.

The Escorial

(for Philip II)

The strict sharp lines and bare facades
Preserve the story of the man
No longer father but the king
To his rebellious, vicious son,

A nocturne sounding deep within
And fading on the outer wall.
Perhaps he watched across the plains
And saw the light-drowned beech trees turn

Into smooth-masted, green-sailed ships,
Imagining the treasure fleet
From half-way round the world had sunk
Again in waters close to home,

Mindful of how the sun could tease
By resting on the bordering hill-
Tops as a tribute all in gold,
Then setting on the other side.

Toledo

1

The eye seeks something to make whole
The city's strangely varied world
In iron stone brick and coloured tile,

The work of Muslim, Christian, Jew,
And settles on a thinning church
Spire vanishing into the blue.

2

Here God is slyly courted with
Cathedral arches looking sky-
Wards cut to take a key and lead
To rooms mosaically adorned,

Contriving with abstractions to
Mirror and hold Him fast, while monks
Lure even closer, singing praise
Until they've trapped Him in their hearts.

3

The inbred, refined images
Of Ferdinand and Isabel,
Called 'their most catholic majesties',
Are everywhere as public art,

The royal initials intertwined
Among great eagles, castles, shields,
With Christ as crown of thorns and cross,
Rod scourge bent nails and spear-pierced heart.

Hurled headlong, jutting out stiff-legged,
The Devil as a gargoyle leers
And streams with water from his crotch,
While in an Inquisition scene

The arrogantly passionate
Fanatic priests and blue bloods are
Like El Greco portrayed, and seem
Pinch-faced to quiver, pale with rage.

4

From on the mediaeval wall
Above the river, unsure if
What's glinting, floating broken up,
Is ice, or something man-made, we

Observe new-age knights speeding round
The corners leading to the bridge
At either end. Their vizors down,
Steeds gleaming, pennons flying taut,

Steel kneecaps sparking, plastic gear
Puffed out and buckling as though they,
Despite no lances, will still be
Unhorsed, we share a knowing look.

5

A freak wind formed, from papers, leaves,
The heavens in the front yard of
A home for spastics, beneath which
They whirled too, in harmony with
An uncoordinated sky,

As happy as they'll ever be,
Perhaps. And then it dropped and left
Them in the lurch with giddiness
To do the same and fall, with all
The other bodies to the ground.

6

Depressed, alone, or, as we say,
'Like death warmed up', I let an old
Sick man for company, and in
A foreign tongue I didn't know,

Earn Charon's coin by guiding me
Around a cemetery packed cheek
By jowl, whose drooping, drained, dust-filmed,
Pale yellow cypresses and pines

Were fitting canopies for graves,
Imagining that he explained
How all the damaged statues of
Christ crucified with at least one

Unnailed limb hanging limply meant
He didn't rise, and how the Grim
Reaper himself, work done too well,
Came in from loneliness and died.

7

(After El Greco's *Christ Driving Out the Money Traders*)

Lined up and open to the sky,
The arches and the temple door
Train glaring light to enter through

The back of Christ's head at full bore.
The money merchants scramble out
And scatter gold coin like hot coals,

Their hands flung up to guard less from
The crinkly three-tailed whip He wields
Than from His bloodshot, God-fired eye.

8

Close to the river's surface, birds
As sunlit-white as holy doves
With their shadows and reflections
Search for fish, flutter swiftly to
A hovering halt when found. Then wings

Drawn tightly in dive bullet-straight,
Concentrated to three-in-one,
As I aspire to focus self,
Streamline, intensify the hunt
Through consciousness to hook a poem.

Avila

1

The mutilated and the poor
Move round the city with the sun
And little else to keep them warm,

While time softens cathedral stone,
Plucks eagles bald and breaks the wings
Off Saint Teresa's doves in flight.

2

A fine day show up broken teeth,
Club feet, ten thumbs and squinting eyes,
The signs of underprivileged genes.
Such people built the city walls,

Served church and king in countless wars.
The past has much to answer for
When sunlight's only kind to stained
Glass windows and bejewelled swords.

3

(After some stone reliefs depicting St Teresa's good works)

In traveller's cloak and hood, her staff
With leaves a simple Tree of Life,
Teresa is seen going forth,
Humble, kindly, happy and sad,
Determined to nourish with love

A land that's resistant to change,
That's arrogant, cynical, cruel,
Defeated and turning the knife in the wound.
A lone starving dog limps howling across
A river bed dry as a bone.

4

An imitation countryside
In concrete holds the animals,
Piped music overlays their sounds
And dust the sleekness of their coats,

As lifelessly, on terraces
Like sideshow shelves, they stand and beg,
With big brown Bambi-target eyes,
To be the first to win the prize.

For St John of the Cross, Segovia

Around the Convent of St John
It's still the dark night of the soul
With ravens jetting in and out
Of crannies in a flesh-hued cliff,

Or else, watchful as hangmen's hoods
They perch in lopped bare trees below,
Though with the crevices as black
As them they seem not to have left,

As if they're decoys to deter
The flocks of heavenly-white doves
That like flurries of snow descend
And braving the illusion soothe

And briefly heal before real guards
Cacophonously chase them off,
A scene of wounded Earth that he
In poems saw as Christ crucified,

Despairing and concluding that
Should He return we'd once again
Drive nails as straight and swiftly in
As black birds here to this day fly.

Seven

Istanbul

1

The rose, stiff pricks and flashing knives,
Stale sweat, gold teeth and signet rings,
Great oafs of men and subtle thieves,

The waterfront charms like Genet,
As clumsy shy and beautiful
As a lorry load of flowers.

2

Nearly three thousand years of age,
It staggers on as improvised,
With heaped up crumbling homes for hordes
That smell of chemicals and drains

To the unaccustomed nose.
God's everything. Men let each other down.
The muezzins in anguish call,
Insisting on the power of prayer.

3

The nomad strain asserts itself
In buildings thrown up overnight,
Reduced to rubble in a year,

In cows and sheep that cross the streets
Against the lights in search of grass.
Why build to last when nothing does?

4

Like pre-war Chevrolet and Dodge,
The city somehow functions still
And only seems to fall apart,

Rust-coloured armour-plated roach
And side-swiped slinking dog with mange
Fit symbols for a coat of arms.

5

We met the dog at every turn,
A threadbare piece of rotting rug
That dodged and trotted, hurried on,
At home among the seething crowds
Of ill-dressed men with frantic eyes,

As though it might outrun its flesh,
The blood-flushed itch it couldn't scratch
As restlessly it circled round
The city like the ruined walls
Where half a million live in holes.

6

(Taksim)

Among the cheap, small-roomed hotels
Stuffed full of sweating, fat men who
Raped Lawrence of Arabia,
The outdoor café with the rose-
Fringed, lace-embroidered tablecloths,

Three-legged, spindly, wrought iron chairs
And awning stripes as faint as on
A well-sucked candy is a breath
Of flesh-free air, as are the cute,
Doll-waitresses, whose masks of make-

Up lend a touch of ritual.
In miniskirts and salmon-pink
Waistcoats they serve herb-flavoured teas
And one-leaf lettuce salads, French-
Dressed lightly, if at all. Inside,

Between Lehar and Strauss, the white-
Tuxedoed pianist dabs at crumbs
And leaves the cake, like Chopin, coughs
In tune with what he plays, and since
The health-food menu's logo's more

A primly sniffing diplomat
Of yore than naughty-ninetie's rake
With top hat monocle and cane,
I wonder if the pretty girls
Spray perfume on the pavement turds.

Through the Eyes of Gallipoli

1

The snow as it falls is blackened by smoke.
Structures of concrete splotch Ataturk Boulevard,
Terraced ones goose-step the hills. The air is of Jews,
Of Greeks who darkened the sky over Smyrna.

At the Bayram sheep are beheaded and flayed
In the streets. Blood prints sheets of ice
With the story of the ram in the thicket.
Infidels burrow chin-deep in their scarves.

2

On a windswept Ataturk-Rides-
Again-Day, a red, one-star sky
With crescent moon fell in as flags
Showered crowds with blood and shrapnel, whirled

Them drowned and glinting, broken-boned,
Down streets they made like our insides
Forever in a state of flux,
While buildings poked out tongues, spat teeth,

And Death in sodden bandages
Kaleidoscopically stripteased,
Waved medals hung with ribbons in
The faces of the casualties.

3

'The Christian and Islamic worlds
Here harmonise,' the Turkish guide
Facetiously intoned and smirked,
Provocatively squatting in

Hobnail boots near Byzantine tiles,
With dirt-choked sponge wiping them to
A blur, fly open for a twist
Of shirt to poke through and evoke

His uncircumcised state, my thought
Flashed like a remedying knife,
Then hatched from mosque domes piglets that
Would never ever fly away.

4

O Istanbul, city of hate
That once threatened Europe and taught
Australians the meaning of war,
I feared your sharp blood-spilling looks

In folk-seething Istikal Mall,
Whose tall buildings either side made
A deep sunless valley of death
For trams shaped like coffins to clear.

O Istanbul, city of thieves,
Who toppled me, yanking hard on
My shoulder-bag strap from behind,
It left me badly skun and bruised

My ego as well, though they fled
Empty-handed, my grip intact.
O Istanbul, city of smiles
The lonely man reads as a sign

That here surely love will solve all,
Mysterious panic attacks
At first drove me back as I crossed
The Galata Bridge to Taksim

And pretty girls advertised in
The English-language rag. And when
At last I'd conquered fear and found
A welcome, I felt as I paid,

And soft brown eyes turned cold and hard,
That you, at rock-bottom, were my
Inherited enemy still.
O Istanbul, city of grief,

Of my soul's resounding defeat,
I longed for my stay to expire
And spent the last days among Greeks
Isolated in The Phanar.*

*The Phanar is the dwindling and sometimes endangered Greek district in Istanbul.

Three Hittite Kings

1

(Tudhaliyas I)

The king is built to the shoulder height of his god
In the mortuary shrine at Yazilikaya.
Together they grew from the hardest of stone
And walk like those who know the terrain:

Sharruma protects and guides, sweeps along
With a friend who kept their enemy clear
Of the shrines. Tudhaliyas walks with his god.
It is a covenant made out of rock.

2

(Suppuliuliumas II)

No letters have come to encourage me here.
Why should they? Alliances shift with events.
I tour a city raised twice from its ruins,
Chariot wheels mud-heavy as the hearts

Of my forebears who waited for allies to come.
A strip of snow grows firm in the cold,
Unwinking crystals, a phalanx of light that glares:
The one skid left, god-given for enemy feet.

3

(Hattusilis I)

All wounds must heal towards the last.
My grandson Mursilis I name
And give as king to this hard land.
The others of my blood have failed

And listened to the serpent's tongue,
The women at the court who turned
Each rock-fast covenant to sand
When I went forth with men-at-arms.

O Tawananna, wife and queen,
Complete your woman's work with me:
Anoint my corpse and hold me close,
Then give me broken back to earth.

Eight

With James McAuley and Georg Trakl in Vienna

1

You said I'd be there at the end,
And so I am, if that meant in
Vienna in the autumn, late
In life and restless still as you

Were searching history-rotten streets
And suppurating parks for poems,
That like those of Georg Trakl show
The soul-destroying decadence,

Despair and evil of the times.
Your works and his with me as friends,
I sit beneath Beethoven's bust
That with its 'Ode to Joy' visage

Would triumphantly dismiss them,
And honouring the truth the shit-
Brown leaves swarming my feet suggest
Defiantly read till it's dark.

2

(Hofburg Palace Gardens)

Sculptured Homeric scenes of war,
Grim double-headed eagles, lions,
Great-bollocked, rearing horses, kings
Astride to show who rules, provided
The monumental milieu for

A rally where the populist
Georg Haider harangues hordes with what
They want to hear, plans that will kill
Time hanging heavily on hands
Familiar with more active use.

It goose-pimples skins leathery as
A crocodile's, tenses up slack
Old buttocks, while march-music stirs,
Blurs eyes that run the flag's two strips
Of red into the one of white,

Provoking memories of 'Sieg Heil!'
Nor am I, passing through by chance
As madness climaxed in the need
For police, proof against the blood's
Wild call threatening to sweep away,

A risk that led in this case to
A sublimation of the worst,
To you imagined by my side
With that other Georg, Trakl,
Admiring Paris hoisting high

'Blonde Helen', his 'opulent freight',
Images from a poem of yours
Translated freely from his work
That always managed to transcend
And transform evil into art.

3

I've come to fancy that a snap
Of Trakl in a book of his
I'm mostly reading in an old
World Viennese coffee house where
He might have sat mirrors my own

Anxious regard. Since after all
We have in common sister-love,
A mother cold as porcelain,
Drug addiction and poetry
That's therapy as well as art.

Hotel Terminus, Vienna

Unspeakable's the word for it,
The noise at dawn each time I stay
At Hotel Terminus, right in

The city's heart. This mix of moan,
Roar whimper scream and sigh gulped down,
The manager is sure, as though

I'm half-witted for having asked,
Is nothing more than pigeons round
The trash bins in the kitchen yard.

But even so, from the eighth floor,
That otherwise is perfect for
A good night's sleep, this sound, which as

It startles me awake and has
Me fighting to set my thoughts straight,
Can only come from souls in hell,

And is the same that I have heard
Underpinning Beethoven's work
And Mozart's music for the dead.

Vienna

Though gods in chariots ride round
The monumental buildings' roofs
To oversee guard bless and save
The city from itself, the main
Impression is they've failed. In white,

No doubt to signify the soul,
The public statue of Mozart
Renders him sugar-sickly, fey,
Effetely civilised and decked-
Out with baroque accessories,

Like convoluted tinsel, more
At home as ornament upon
A *Sachertorte*, the national sweet,
While Beethoven, a bust beside
A car park only seems to say

'Thank God I'm deaf!' The final stars,
Schiele, Wittgenstein, Kokoschka, Zweig,
Klimt, Mahler, Musil, Rilke, Freud,
Are in quintessence to be found
In Georg Trakl's poetry

Of decadence decay and death,
As pathologically disturbed,
Obsessed with suicide and sex,
Culturally confirming Franz
Joseph, the emperor, in defeat:

A horseless, life-size bronze consigned
To a far corner of a park,
No medals on his uniform,
He stands alone, stooped, frail and old,
Head bowed and turning green to boot.

Rembrandt's Self-portraits in Vienna

One on the edge of tears, he paints
Exactly what he feels, not vague,
Sad atmospheres of loneliness,
Depression and the fear of hell.
Another, bankrupt, says 'Don't touch',

And shrinks into the dark. A third
Appeals, asks if it's fair that he,
No murderer, thief, should also be
Like them, punished, disgraced, right down
To the details even of worms?

After a Painting by Matisse

Perhaps the violinist on
The balcony, playing, it seems,
To the pink-shaded sky, is Death
On holiday, his trademark face

A mask turned to his occiput.
But since it's looking at, behind
Him in the near-foreground, a warm,
Lived-in, yet weirdly empty room,

That he as Janus could have cleared
Of people recently, best push
Him off to make quite sure. And aren't
They nightfall's rather than dawn's hues?

Not to mention what's out of sight:
The possibility of streets
Below in which the celebrants
Of carnival are lying dead.

Mediaeval German Christs

(Dahlem Museum, Berlin)

Not immaculately conceived,
Since uninspired, dutifully done,
The Christs seem comic, wooden in
The wood five roomfuls of His Life

Were carved from. Squirming, windy babes
Become as fat as mud, then too
Old plausibly to rise from bed,
Let alone the dead, they have leers

For smiles displaying Goofy teeth
Jan Brueghel would have surely sunk
Into breast or cross, not left as
The sign of an unworthy hand.

Nine

Former Czech Communist Boss

The concrete benches, heavy as
A Brezhnev frown, their backs turned on
Flower beds cut into his and chill
The kidneys, though he ordered them

For public places, where he now,
Habitué of parks and squares,
Must shift, as he's learned history can,
His limbs, constantly searching for

Temporary comfort, and which,
Occasionally, briefly bring,
In a new contortion, the look
Of hammer and sickle to mind.

Or else he paces, biting hard
Upon the pain of his defeat,
As if breaking through teeth might ease
The wound, that does indeed give way,

At length, to a dull warming mood
Of self-pity, in which he views
As honourable the daily drudge
Of loneliness, as something that

At least will last! As for the rest,
Dialectical, godless skills
Always enable him to prove
That life's as meaningless as his,

That there's nothing to miss out on,
And thus consoled he'll soundly sleep,
As every night, joyously in
Anticipation of the grave.

Czech Republic

As I travelled the countryside
Following communism's fall,
I was struck by the damage half
A century of neglect had done

To statues of Christ crucified.
Thick lichen, missing faces, limbs,
Could make them difficult to pick,
And even though, against the odds,

He often clung for dear life to
A broken bit of Cross, His man-
Forged tree, it was sun's splintering light
Transfiguring the clusters of

Red rowan berries spread like flesh
Throughout the branches which meant He'd
Always, regardless of art's fate,
Survive the horrors of the times.

Czech Concert

The first violinist, winking, inviting,
Lured me to camp it up,
Indulge in an exchange of mock
Heroic sentiments as he
Led gaily in a flash black tux

And shiny pumps, twinkle-toed like
Mephisto through Beethoven, Bach,
Mozart and Brahms, making light of
Europe's pure high seriousness
In art. But at drinks afterwards

With an audience dressed to hear
The best, he came in T-shirt, jeans
And red trainers, which in polite
Post-communist society
Identified him as a pimp,

A lesser mafioso they
All pointedly ignored. And when,
Because we'd at least shared a joke,
No matter how much in bad taste,
I offered him my hand, his blank

Regard as an accompaniment
To it left in mid-air obliged
Me publicly to listen to
An inner work perhaps best named
'Cacophony of Rage and Shame'.

Jack the Ripper in Prague

(for Jakub Schikaneder (1855–1924))

I love the streets at night when they
Gleam stickily, wet from light rain,
And Schikaneder, brush dipped in
The darkness could have painted them,

When in my mind's eye I replace
The cars with his signature coach
That sinisterly seems to wait
In so much of his work for Jack

The Ripper to emerge from out
Of blackest nowhere, and whom I
Supply as myself fastening up
A Gladstone bag in nervous haste.

O I could eat the city then,
So happy do I feel, at home,
Because I can afford at last
To drop my vigilance and be

Relaxed about this aspect of
My soul, the phobia that I
Was born to kill the fairer sex.
Since he, a fellow-artist, lived

Obsessed by scenes implicit with
This worst of possibilities
And died at seventy without
A murdered woman to his name.

Winter Walk, Hradec Králové

Like a grey corpse, the river lay
Frozen from bend to bend no red-
Scarfed skater sped around to save
From definitive cheerlessness,
From thoughts of death beyond recall,

Unless the solitary black bird,
Of 'one for sorrow, two for joy'
Renown, croaked false, risking its beak
To break the rigor mortis grip
Of ice for live fish just below.

Ten

Constitutional

(George's Bay, St Helens, Tasmania)

A thrilling elegance of curve
Seductive as a woman's hip
Thrust out, a corner on the track

Skirting the bay is blind and brings
The black stampeded horses of
Hippolytus as suddenly

To mind as they might sweep around
And trample, and of course the train
On top of Tolstoy's heroine

Before she knew it, and Nietzsche,
Who without warning on a bend,
Confronted by a rearing mare

Being mercilessly flogged, flung
His arm about her and went mad.
And so I bypass on my walk

A bench located there, my gran-
Dad resting on one having been
Out of the blue struck down by death.

Dance of Death: Binalong Bay

Walking one night across a soft,
Treacherously uneven beach,
Jarred, shaken up to the extent
Of impending dislocation,
I felt my skeleton was on

The brink of getting out, though not
Cleanly and smoothly, all at once,
But bit by bit, obtruding like
A sharp-edged, ragged patchwork quilt
Of rock from underneath sand it

Was not able to quite throw off.
As Hamlet couldn't thaw and melt,
Dissolve his flesh into a dew
And had to stay, partially at least,
Encumbered and in tatters dressed,

Mine too would not permit a dance
All neat and tidy in one piece
With moonlight starring elbows, knees
And other angularities,
Finally to take a bow and fall

Together in a compact heap.
It was, rather, to be a mess,
A widespread scattering of bones
In keeping with the life I've led,
Mostly in mental anarchy,

Freebooting as a cannon on
The loose in countries round the globe,
Disoriented, dispossessed,
A meaningless dispersal save
For poetry that structures me.

Memento Mori at Seventy-eight

So clearly head of table is
The loudly tick-tocking wall clock
At shoulder height above it that
No one else thinks of sitting there,

Afraid of what it represents,
As on and on, insatiably,
It chomps away at life, its food,
A noisily ill-mannered guest

We don't recall inviting, but
Who can't be easily ignored,
A bully boy who dominates
With monologues on death and won't

Allow me any peace at meals,
Staring rudely until I hear
'Begone, you've not much left of me
In which to write a timeless poem!'

East Coast, Tasmania (2)

(for Nick and Sally Evers)

1

Still water for a time became
A gallery with replicas
Of clouds and trees,

Frayed edges, subtle twists
And splintered bark removed
As in a glossy photograph,

Smooth-textured undulations
Of sand pink-pricked with light
Weak versions of a cliff,

Its clumsily protruding rocks
And face slashed by the sun
Made bearable to human eyes.

I stoned the pool to frosted glass:
Replicas had disappeared,
Originals remained.

2

Kelp, cowrie, limpet, she-oak, pig
Face, Black Boy strangers to my touch,
Dark sea more ruffled as I look,
The dunes confusing with new shapes,

Gulls screaming as they leave their food,
The dotterels always on ahead,
Because long absence can't be bridged
By knowing just the proper names.

3

Pied oyster fledglings take their rest
After the terrors of a flight
Above huge hissing, feathery waves

Lent monstrous wings by passing clouds,
The look and noise softened as they
Bask in sunlight behind ridged sand.

4

Brown shrivelled, lightweight, worm-drilled wood
The dead, knots joints and organs, bits
Left over from canopic jars
And mummies, wave-piled stones robbed tombs,

And cracks the streets that run between,
As in old age we note as well
Birds printing sand around the mound
With hieroglyphs to keep it safe.

5

Among the cracked and spidery rocks,
Sea fussing over them with lace,
The day is like old maiden aunts,

The seagulls gossiping in groups,
Crabs scuttling at the smallest sound,
Clefts faintly trickling, slightly sour.

6

Light blue and hazy as a dream,
The hills seemed worn away, as though
A rending of the veil would show
Sky's nothing waiting to be sown

With hope, when suddenly, between
One heartbeat and the next, sand blew,
Stung skin and blinded, blanketing
And walling off the God we seek.

www.ingramcontent.com/pod-product-compliance
Lightning Source LLC
Chambersburg PA
CBHW070925080526
44589CB00013B/1432